GW01605465

SCIURUS

The Story of a Grey Squirrel

COLLINS ANIMAL LIVES

Other books in the series

TALPA The Story of a Mole
KENNETH MELLANBY

VULPINA The Story of a Fox
DAVID MACDONALD

CAPREOLUS The Story of a Roe Deer
RAYMOND E. CHAPLIN

LUTRA The Story of an Otter *(coming shortly)*
PHILIP WAYRE

SCIURUS

The Story of a Grey Squirrel

JAN TAYLOR

Illustrated by Harold George

COLLINS
ST JAMES'S PLACE · LONDON

William Collins Sons & Co Ltd
London · Glasgow · Sydney · Auckland
Toronto · Johannesburg

First published 1978

ISBN 0 00 195743 0
Made and Printed in Great Britain
by W & J Mackay Ltd. Chatham

Contents

To Ross, Graham and Jonathan

Foreword

Sciurus (pronounced: ski-yurus, both "u"s as in puss or bull) is the story of a grey squirrel who lives in woodlands nearWindsor Park. It is not a real life story because I would have to be a squirrel myself to experience all the day to day happenings in a wild animal's life. As a human observer in these woodlands I felt I was doing well if I caught a brief view of any individual squirrel more than once a week, which is a very small glimpse into its real life. On the other hand, each day I went into the woodlands, I saw a lot of different squirrels and carefully recorded the things I saw them do and what happened to them. I have brought together in *Sciurus* some of these notes which I hope give a true impression of the sort of life a squirrel leads.

The life of a squirrel may be as different from the next squirrel as my life is different from yours, but all squirrels are likely to experience similar happenings. They, like Sciurus, will have to escape from predators, learn how to open nuts, and how to establish social relationships with other squirrels.

I have described only a few events in Sciurus's first year of life. I would need to write a long book if I were to complete his life story, because Sciurus lives in a world where social strife is ever present and where death is commonplace. About ten squirrels die for every one that survives long enough to have a family of its own. Every day is filled with events which we might regard as exciting or fearful, but to Sciurus they may hardly be worth noting. We, of course, do not know how a squirrel may feel about any of these events, such as being struck by a sparrowhawk, or seeing snow for the first time. I think it probable that some behaviour can rightly be interpreted as showing fear, hunger, frustration and contentment, but for the most part I leave Sciurus's feelings to your own imagination.

I have chosen the name "Sciurus" because that is the scientific name given to all kinds of squirrels by the great Swedish naturalist, Carl von Linne. Like other scientific names, it is in Latin, but originally Aristotle made the name up from two Greek words meaning "shade-tail". The grey squirrel's full scientific name, given to it in 1788 by Johann Gmelin, is *sciurus carolinensis* – "shade-tail from Carolina". This is because he knew that its natural home was on the eastern side of America, especially in the states of North and South Carolina. In 1876 grey squirrels were first successfully released in Great Britain. They soon spread over much of the country because the habitat was suitable and easy to invade by means of interconnecting hedgerows. Also most of their natural predators and diseases were left behind in America; only the fleas which plague Sciurus, and a few other organisms, were accidentally introduced at the same time as the squirrels.

Squirrel populations in England now seem to be relatively large and variable compared to those in America, partly because they lack these natural causes of death and partly because the English woodlands and plantations are smaller and do not have the variety of trees found in America. These factors contribute to the appearance of a new and worrying behaviour found in the English grey squirrels. They strip living bark from trees in some woodlands to such an extent that many trees become deformed or die. *Sciurus* includes some bark-stripping episodes in which I piece together the probable causes of this behaviour. It forms part of the complex sign language which squirrels normally use. But, in the conditions found in Britain which differ so much from America, stray squirrels may converge on plantations during early summer, use this aggressive signal to excess, and eat the bark in the process. Squirrels use many other signals in their language though it is often difficult to be sure of their meaning. I have interpreted them as best I can for you.

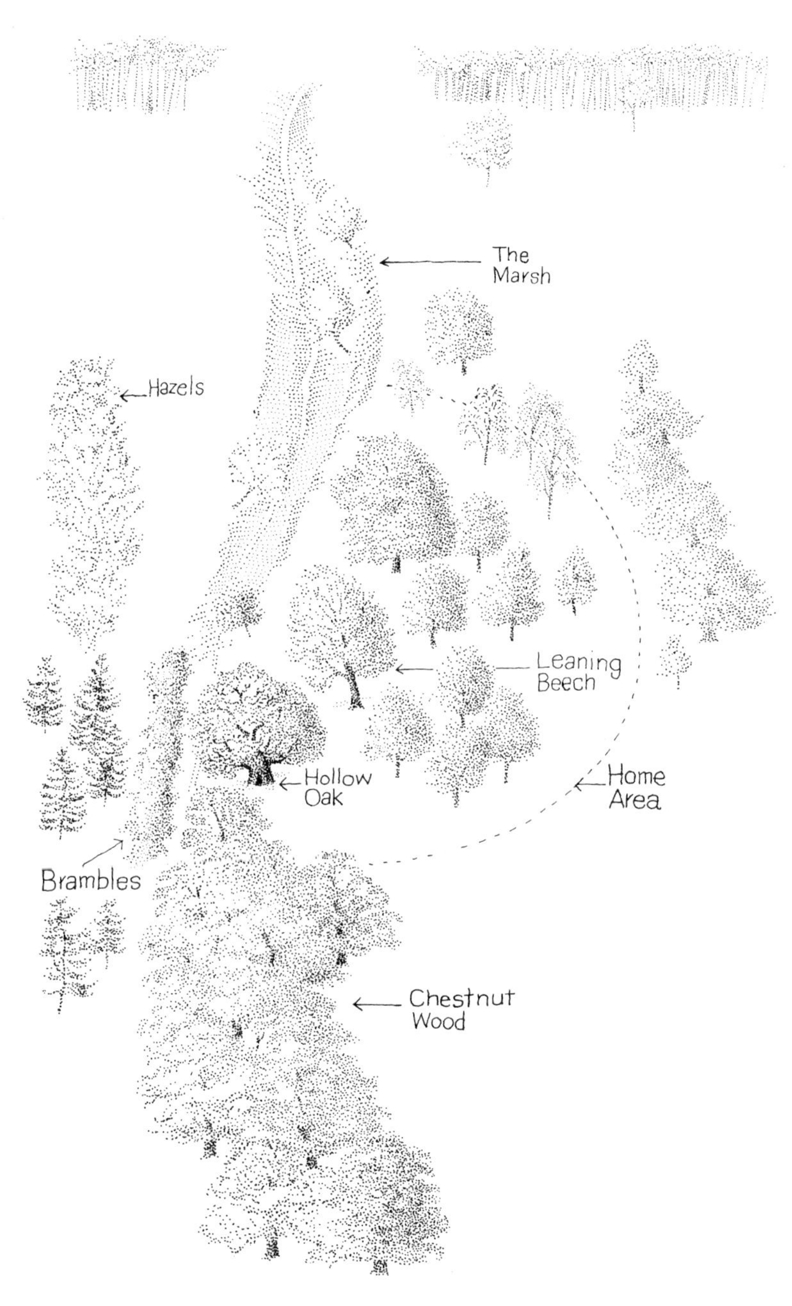
The Marsh
Hazels
Leaning Beech
Hollow Oak
Home Area
Brambles
Chestnut Wood

I

Sciurus Wakes Up

Sciurus woke with a start; something strange had given him a fright. He knew very little about the world because he was only thirty-two days old, but he was using his senses and learning fast. He could feel the cool air coming in through the entrance hole of the nest in the tree trunk, and the warm bodies of his brother and sister. He was used to the senses of smell and touch and a week ago he had begun to hear things properly when his ears opened. Now on this September morning he had been awakened by the piercing alarm call of a blackbird. This had frightened him and he cowered down in the nest close to his brother and sister. But he soon realized he was receiving a new sensation. Light and strange pictures appeared

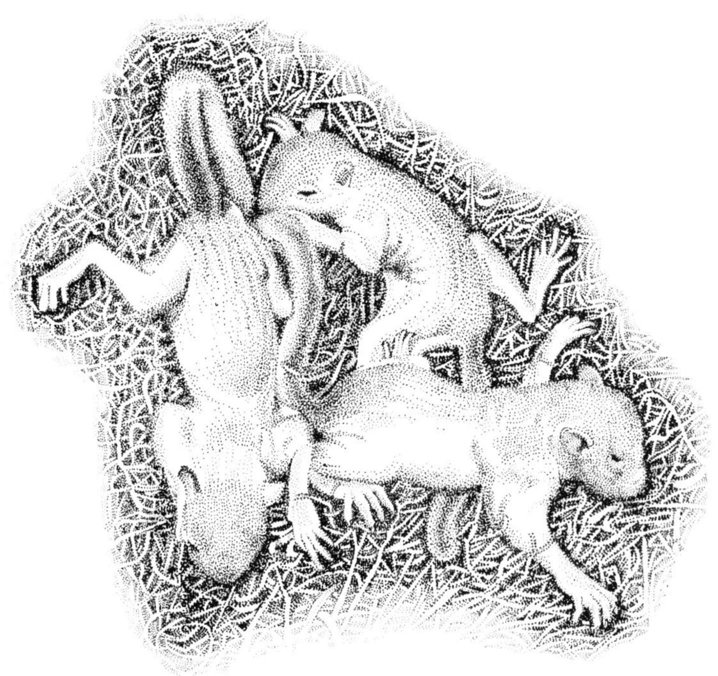

through one misty eye which had just opened for the first time.

His mother was in the branches of the next tree, splitting beechnuts open and eating the soft kernels inside. She froze when she heard the blackbird and dropped the nut she was holding. The nut fell, clacking through layers of green leaves, to the woodland floor. She could hear the noise of an animal running over the dead leaves on the ground, and then a scraping sound as it climbed the slippery trunk of the leaning beech tree. This was the tree where Sciurus was cowering in the nest. The tree had been struck by lightning a long time ago, which had made a spiral gash in the trunk, and a woodpecker had used the gash to make a nest-hole. Generations of squirrels had lived in the hole after this, and in the course of time fungus had rotted the trunk until the nest merely lay at the bottom of a cavern in the tree trunk.

Suddenly Sciurus's mother saw that the animal was a stoat. There was little she could do except watch. The stoat rushed up to the first branch of the tree, sniffed around and then went higher to an old summer drey, lodged in a hollow where a branch had fallen off. (Squirrels' leaf nests are often called dreys.) The stoat went into the drey for a moment, then came out and looked up towards the hole. It started to climb the spiral gash, but then turned and ran down the tree and began hunting for rabbits, its normal prey.

It was a lucky escape for Sciurus, but he was not aware of the drama taking place outside. All he knew was that he was beginning to feel hungry. His mother did not return to the nest for a long time, in case the stoat saw her. Sciurus became so hungry that he started making piercing squeals, and these finally brought his mother back.

She nuzzled all three babies, reassuring them. They began searching for her teats by feel and smell, fighting with each other for their favour-

ite positions. They soon needed to urinate but were still too young to go outside, so in order to keep the nest clean their mother licked them all in turn and swallowed their waste.

After the baby squirrels had fed for a while, their mother became agitated, especially when Sciurus accidentally nipped her teat with his new incisor teeth. She picked Sciurus up, holding him in her mouth round the middle. He automatically curled himself round her neck, and he could dimly see, through his one open eye, what was happening. She carried her heavy bundle out of the hole into the blinding daylight and down the slippery trunk.

Sciurus's mother took him across the wood-

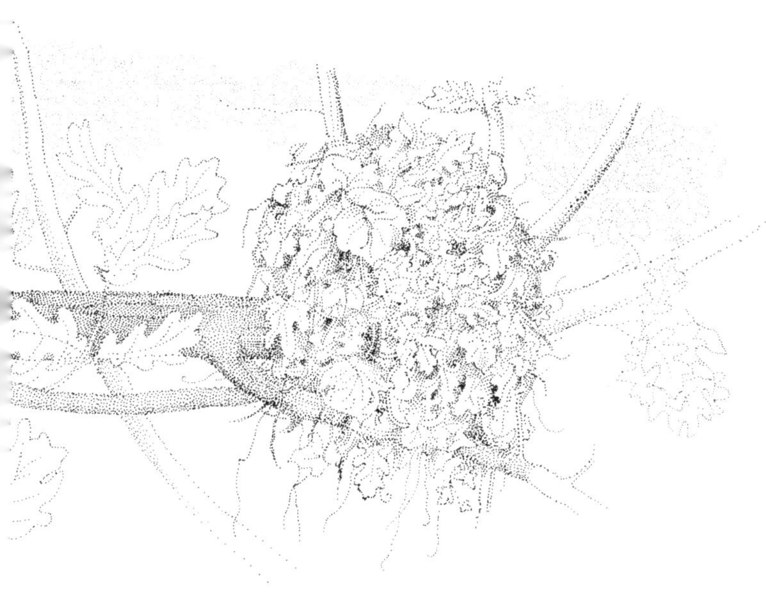

land floor to a large oak tree and climbed up its craggy bark, which was much easier than climbing the smooth trunk of the beech. She stopped at the top of the trunk, where it divided into three large branches, and Sciurus had a glimpse of their new home. It was a drey made of leafy twigs, now dead and shrivelled up. From the outside it looked like a large, rounded pile of leaves, but when his mother took Sciurus in through a concealed opening he found it was soft inside. His mother had made a nest inside the leafy twigs; it was about the size of a football, and was lined with honeysuckle bark and dried grasses, shredded into soft strips by her teeth. She had made this nest before Sciurus was born in case she needed to move the family.

While his mother went off to collect the other two young, Sciurus had time to explore his new surroundings. He was very unsteady on his feet because he was unused to walking. When he was born at the beginning of August he had been almost helpless. Then he had been about ten centimetres long to the tip of his tail, and hairless except for some whiskers. He weighed only fifteen grammes and could do little else but struggle, find his mother's teats and squeak when distressed. Now he was six times as heavy, twenty-five centimetres long and had a silvery-grey coat. He tried to explore the drey, using all his senses. The problem was to stand up, but his big feet wouldn't stay where they were supposed to.

Shakily he moved forward, but rolled over on his side because one leg hadn't moved in time. He got up and had another try, and this time he stayed the right way up. He made little purring noises as he moved forward again. He could see some of the nesting materials in the light that came through the opening, and he could feel and smell objects on the floor of the drey. He bit a twig with his incisor teeth to discover what it was made of. It tasted bitter and felt hard. Warily he moved a bit farther and stumbled on to something which smelled different. When he tried to grasp it with his teeth, it moved away. He became excited and purred loudly as he reached forward to try again. It was an earwig; it tweaked his nose and made Sciurus squeal and fall over. Luckily it was not a centipede, which has a poisonous bite and often lives in the base of squirrels' dreys.

The next moment his mother brought his sister in through the entrance and dumped her in the bottom of the drey. The two babies, attracted by each other's warm bodies, clambered over one another and were fast asleep together when their mother brought the last of her family in through the entrance hole.

2

The Outside World

Two weeks had passed since his encounter with the earwig, and Sciurus had grown into an alert little squirrel. He was able to see properly with both his eyes. Now he was sleeping in the drey, being gently rocked as the oak branches waved in the breeze. When he began to wake up at ten o'clock in the morning, he nuzzled around sleepily, looking for his mother's teats, unaware that she had gone out an hour ago and was busy up in the trees eating green acorns. First he tried sucking his fingers, but this wasn't quite right, so he nuzzled a bit farther and found his sister's toes. As she pulled her feet away, Sciurus opened his eyes and woke sufficiently to preen her fur with his long front teeth instead. All three were awake now, and Sciurus tried to catch some fleas while preening his sister. He was not very good at it yet. While trying to comb one out he nipped his sister's skin. She flicked round and struck out with her forepaws making a loud squeaking growl. This set them all romping and playing with one another in the nest until Sciurus popped his head out of the entrance hole.

During the previous few days he had looked out of the drey entrance from time to time, and had been outside twice, clambering over the branches and getting used to climbing. He now seemed to be in a more adventurous mood. It was a warm sunlit day and a gentle breeze was blowing. He crawled out of the drey on to a small branch and squatted sideways on it trying to stay on top while the others came out. His brother still felt like romping and began to climb on top of Sciurus. This was a bit risky because there was a six metre drop to the ground below the branch. Sciurus sat up and tried to push him off with his forepaw, but lost his balance and toppled over, head first, towards the ground. But he saved himself instinctively by hanging on to the branch with his hind feet, and merely swung round below the branch. He ran back to the trunk under his brother, flapping his silvery tail to keep his balance. Once there he came back at his brother on top of the branch again, but each time he got nearer to getting his revenge, his brother hopped across to the next branch. Sciurus gnawed a chunk out of the tree's bark, as if feeling frustrated, but was soon distracted by something on an oak leaf.

He climbed along the branch to a group of leafy twigs, then stretched up with his nose to the object and pulled it off with his teeth. He sat down on his haunches, steadying himself with his elbows, because he had not yet learned how to sit up in a proper squirrel manner. He held his find in his forepaws; it was round and as big as a marble, pale green on one side and pink on the other. He turned it round in his paws, sniffing it all over, then bit a chunk out of it. It was quite soft, but when he drew it back in his mouth to his chewing teeth he found it tasted horrid, so he threw his nose in the air, and pushed the bits out with his tongue. Not put off by this experience, he continued to bite bits off and drop them without tasting them. In the middle of the cherry gall he found a harder lump which broke quite easily. Inside was the soft tasty maggot of the insect which had made the gall. He was now finding out which things were good to eat. He would soon have to learn to fend for himself, because in the next few weeks he would be weaned off

his mother's milk.

When he had eaten the maggot he dropped the rest of the gall. It made a crash when it fell on some dry leaves. Sciurus heard the noise and looked down. The woodland floor looked interesting so he went down to investigate.

He began climbing down the trunk backwards, which proved to be very awkward. It was easy climbing upwards because all his claws hooked into the bark, but his feet seemed to be the wrong way round to go down head first. But then he found his ankles were double-jointed so that his feet twisted round behind him and he could hang head down from his claws. Even his wrists turned to allow his

claws to grip the bark, so it was really quite easy to come down head first. Nevertheless he came down rather slowly.

Eventually he arrived on the ground, and began sniffing around at all the new things he found, while his brother and sister came scraping down the tree, showering him with bits of bark dislodged from the trunk. It was a totally new experience to be on the ground; there was no risk of losing one's grip and falling. So, in between sniffing at bits of beechnut and acorn cup, they chased one another around the tree base, into a cleft between the roots, then amongst some yellowing bracken fronds and birch saplings. Meanwhile their mother had returned and was watching them from above the drey.

Sciurus looked out across the woodland floor and saw another tree trunk some way from his own. It was a beech tree. He stretched towards it with his tail curled over his back, and moved his head from side to side in order to have a good look, in case there was something dangerous around. Then, slowly, he hopped and walked towards it, but had a fright when he suddenly noticed something strange in his path. It was a fly agaric toadstool, bright red on top and flecked with white.

Sciurus had never seen anything like it before

and approached it with great caution. He pushed his tail as far forward as it would go, looped to one side of his head, and was ready to leap away unharmed should his tail be attacked. But the toadstool just stayed there and did nothing. Sciurus sniffed its rim, then put his forefeet on top and smelled some of the white spots. He gouged a bit out with his teeth, and made smacking noises as he tasted it. The fungus still didn't do anything so he tore a big chunk out of it and tried a bit more. It probably didn't taste good enough for him to eat much, so he dropped the rest of it and went to look at the tree.

He was sniffing round its base when a wood-pigeon flew up, clapping its wings. This frightened him and he leaped up on to the tree trunk, but instead of going up the beech, he found he just slipped back down again, leaving long scratch marks in the powdery green algae growing on the smooth bark. Rather than try again, he rushed back to the safety of his oak and rejoined his brother and sister.

They all climbed back up the tree, and Sciurus went out on to the smaller branches again, hoping to find another cherry gall. He found a rounded thing, but this time it was an acorn. He tugged at it, but it didn't come off easily like the gall. Eventually he chewed through the stalk and sat up, holding the acorn still in its cup. He chewed the cup off first and then turned the green acorn round and round in his hands looking for a good point to get his teeth into it, because they kept slipping over the hard shiny coat. They cut into the base first, and he was able to break bits off the seed coat. He tried a bit of the acorn inside and it probably tasted very bitter, because he quickly pushed it out of his mouth. He turned the acorn round and found his teeth sank into the top end where a little spike stuck out. This time when he tried the acorn underneath it tasted much better, almost sweet.

While Sciurus was balancing on the twigs

amongst the leaves and acorns, making these discoveries, something terrible happened. He froze when he heard his mother's soft cough-like warning call, but before he could do anything he heard the whirring sound of feathers tearing the air and coming straight for him. The dark figure of a sparrowhawk shot through the leaves and he was struck on the back by its talons. He grappled and grasped hold of some leaves and twigs in a desperate attempt to save himself. He could feel the heavy push on his back as the hawk tried to knock him off the tree, but just when he thought his claws were going to break free from their hold on the branch, the hawk flew off. Sciurus ran quickly towards the main branch but the hawk swooped again. This time Sciurus had a much firmer grip and there was no risk of his being knocked out of the tree. The hawk gave up and flew away, and Sciurus ran to join his brother and sister in the safety of the drey. His back was sore and bleeding, but his mother soon licked his wounds clean when she returned. Sciurus took comfort from his mother's milk and was much more cautious when he ventured out of the drey again.

3

Nuts and Acorns

It was a dull drizzly day in the middle of October and Sciurus was very busy. His mother now spent very little time with the family and usually slept in the hole in the leaning beech where Sciurus had been born. Sciurus had no need to stay with her now because he had a complete set of teeth and was fully weaned.

He rushed up the oak tree and ran out along a branch amongst the leafy twigs. Clutches of two or three acorns were hanging on pendulous stalks, and while he grabbed hold of an acorn in his teeth, he knocked another out of its cup with his nose. Two more fell and crashed down as he scrambled back to the main branch. Once there, he skilfully gouged out a groove in the top end of the acorn and ate the sweet-tasting growing point inside. Then he ran down the tree, acorn in his mouth, and over the woodland floor until he came to a patch of stumpy grasses. Here he walked slowly, nose to ground, occasionally flicking his bushy tail until he found what seemed to be a good place to store the acorn. He dug a little pit with his forepaws, put the acorn in it, and, putting weight behind

his front teeth, rammed it firmly in place. He raked earth over the acorn and patted it down and then carefully spread some leaf litter on top so that the hiding place would be hard to find.

Having made this store he ran back up the tree for another acorn, and was soon on the ground again, looking for a good spot to bury it. His brother and sister were in the same tree, helping to make the food store for winter, and he could see many other squirrels, especially when they flicked their bushy tails. His brother's tail, like his own, was clearly banded with brown and black and had white streaks up each side. There was so much food around that the squirrels just could not eat it all, so they were busy storing it for later use. Winter was approaching and their lives depended on enough being stored to last them until spring.

Sciurus was looking for a good place to store an acorn amongst some bracken fronds when he got a surprise. His brother was overhead collecting more acorns and one fell and crashed on to some dry leaves near Sciurus under the bracken. Sciurus leaped back in fright, not knowing what it was. He squatted for a moment, flapping his tail vigorously and making a purring sound through his nose. He then ran up the tree, whirling his tail over his back and calling "chuck . . . chuck . . . chuck . . .".

He sat on a low branch and continued calling and jerking his tail while looking intently, turning his head from side to side, to see whether anything moved near where the acorn fell. Every so often he made a hiccoughing "chareeeee . . ." call. Three other squirrels replied, making the same calls, then he heard more calling farther away. He hadn't realized how many squirrels there were until he heard them chorusing like this, and he learned that calling was used as a means of locating other squirrels.

After a while he felt he must get on with the food store, so he climbed up to get another acorn. He was cautious coming down the tree in case the noise caused by the acorn had been made by a stoat or fox in the bracken patch. He continued to call as he came down, but, as he had a mouth full of acorn, his calls sounded muffled – "shwee . . . shwee . . . chaw . . . chaw . . . chaw".

There were now so many acorns on the ground that he often collected these instead of climbing all the way up the tree. Each acorn had a different sort of smell and he soon found that some of the smaller ones were filled with droppings left by beetle larvae. He ignored these because it would have been a waste of time storing beetle-eaten or rotten acorns.

Just then a flock of wood pigeons arrived in the wood, and settled under the beech trees. They walked around picking up beechnuts. Some of them went under the oaks and ate the fallen acorns, including some of the worm-eaten ones. They had no sense of smell so were not able to tell the difference as easily as Sciurus could. They turned some leaves over with their bills, but did not find buried acorns because they were hidden from sight. Sciurus could easily find them by his sense of smell. The bustle of animals and birds all around seemed to make Sciurus frisky and he ran full speed, turning this way and that, with his tail flicking vertically in the air. He kicked off from the base of a small birch sapling and rushed at two wood pigeons. As they clapped out of his way he began to chase some bramblings. These pretty birds are seen in beechwoods only when there are lots of nuts.

When he stopped and had a look around to make sure there was no danger at hand, he saw bushy tails flicking in the air as other squirrels stored acorns. He instantly recognized another squirrel, standing about 15 metres away, as a scruffy young male belonging to the neighbouring family. Sciurus ran over to him, knowing from previous encounters that he would flee. He chased him up an oak tree and the two squirrels made loud scratching noises as they spiralled round the trunk. The young male squeaked when Sciurus bit his tail, then ran across to the next tree, while Sciurus stopped to preen himself, having tired of the chase.

It was a different story when Sciurus came down the tree. A young squirrel six months older than Sciurus saw him. This squirrel always tried to dominate him and this time chased him back up the tree. Sciurus dived into a bolthole in a hollow branch and quickly

turned round to face the incoming squirrel. In this position he squeaked, growled and struck out at its face with foreclaws. The bossy squirrel chattered its teeth and went away.

By chasing and being chased Sciurus was learning about his relationships with other squirrels living in the same part of the wood. He was familiar with them all by now. At least he was until he came out of the bolthole a little later and saw a squirrel he didn't recognize.

Instead of having a brown summer coat, it had the silvery-grey streaks of a growing winter coat on either side of its rump. This squirrel appeared to be uncertain where it was going. Sciurus ran over to have a closer look, but then he was frightened. He saw it was a strange male and he ran away. The stranger started storing acorns, then ran up the tree and called to let the squirrels within hearing know where it was. Other squirrels called to inform it where they all were, and a little later one of the adult males living in the area came into the tree and chased the stranger away aggressively. Sciurus didn't see the stranger for some time. Then it suddenly appeared from behind a tree trunk and ran straight towards Sciurus. Before he knew what was happening the stranger had bitten and torn his ear. Sciurus had to run as if chased by a predator. He ran up a sapling birch with the squirrel hard on his tail and when he was near the top he leaped, spreading out his tail and legs, and escaped by sailing to the ground below. But Sciurus was chased many more times that day by the stranger, the domineering male and by some other squirrels too. He had a piece missing from his ear for the rest of his life.

He went back to the drey that night feeling low. He needed to find a woodland where the squirrels did not chase him and where there was plenty of food for them all. When he woke up the next day he went exploring. He went to the edge of his known world which was marked by a big hollow oak. He had been this far from his circle of beeches only once before, and had never seen any of the other squirrels known to him go past this tree.

Everything seemed strange on the other side. There was a stream running into a marsh overgrown with stinging nettles and willow bushes. He could see trees on the other side so he decided to investigate. He hopped through the stream getting rather wet, but shook himself and sprayed most of the water off. Then he followed a rabbit track through some brambles, eating an over-ripe blackberry on the way. While going through the nettlebed he got stung on the nose, which made him jump. The track

wound about until it came to a small willow tree. Sciurus climbed its trunk and found that he was nearer the trees on the other side, so he came down again and continued following the rabbit track. It came out into an open grassy patch surrounded by rushes where the rabbits had been grazing. He headed for the dark cover of some bushes near an oak tree.

Here Sciurus stopped suddenly. He smelled something very pleasant. It was oval like an acorn, but didn't have the same slippery surface. He picked it up and turned it round looking for somewhere to open it. His teeth rasped the shell but it didn't split open. He tried several places, cutting grooves in the surface, but still it wouldn't crack. It smelled so good that he decided to rasp at it until it did open. His bottom teeth came together to form a sharp cutting chisel, and he rasped away until a deep groove was formed. At last his teeth broke through the shell. He put his teeth through the hole and levered the shell until it broke off in bits and he was able to taste the hazelnut inside. This tasted so good that he stayed there looking for more nuts.

After a while he found another one which didn't smell as nice, and wasn't so heavy. Inside he found nothing but a grub and its droppings. He left the wormy ones alone after this and became quite an expert at opening the nuts by cutting a groove at the top of the shell and then splitting the nut neatly into two halves. There were not many nuts left; squirrels had been eating them long before they ripened and Sciurus was finding the few they had missed. When he couldn't find any more, he climbed the oak. There were thousands of acorns on the tree, but it was too small for building a drey and too young to have any suitable nest-holes.

He went farther along the hedgerow and came to a clump of pine trees where it was dark and eerie. He didn't like these trees at all and ran quickly through them to the edge of the stream again. He was able to cross without getting wet this time as a tree had fallen down a long time ago and its trunk formed a bridge. Across the stream he found another wood. There were some very big trees. Some, like the oaks and beeches, were familiar; others were new to him. One of these had a very large trunk with shaggy bark twisting up in a spiral.

Sciurus pricked his toes on something as he walked under the tree, and found a bigger nut than he had ever seen before. He took this to a stump nearby and chewed open the pointed end in the same way as he was used to with acorns. Inside he found some sweet-tasting flesh. This sweet chestnut was so good that he stripped all the shell off and ate most of the flesh, but he found that it dried up his mouth when he ate some of the base. If he was going to make his home here he must store these nuts, so he busied himself finding them amongst the prickly husks, taking them to the stump to chew out the sweet-tasting top which provided all the food he needed to eat, and then storing them in the same way as he had been doing with the acorns.

Food supplies seemed all right, but what about other squirrels: would they accept him? He began to notice them and felt uneasy. Some youngsters came near him and ran away, then a large adult male appeared. There was no mistaking his intentions: he ran straight at Sciurus. Sciurus wanted to avoid another torn ear but didn't know which way to run. He didn't want to go back into the pine trees, so he ran away blindly through the unfamiliar territory. The male soon lost interest and went back to pick up the chestnut Sciurus had been holding. But before Sciurus could regain his composure another squirrel chased him farther through the wood to some birch trees. He climbed one of these, feeling very miserable. Not only had he been unsuccessful in finding somewhere pleasant to live, but he did not know how to find his way back home.

Luckily, unknown to him, he had been chased most of the way to the circle of beeches which was his home. When he looked out from the top of the tree he could see the hollow oak. This cheered him up and he ran to and fro through the branches of the birch, flicking his tail, and then ran full speed back to the drey.

There he found his brother, and they preened each other. That night his sister didn't return. Sciurus never saw her again. She could have been killed by a cat or some other predator, but it is just possible that, unlike Sciurus, she had found a new place to live.

4

Winter Home

Sciurus was now determined to stay in the area where he was born. He worked very hard storing acorns, making sure that each one was buried separately so that if a bird found one accidentally, only one was lost from the store. He didn't need to remember where the acorns were buried because he could smell them as he walked over the ground. But there were many squirrels living in the area and they couldn't all survive the winter on the food stored. Whenever he could, Sciurus chased the scruffy young squirrel and eventually it disappeared. In time, the domineering squirrel, and some of the others also, either died, killed by predators or disease, or went away looking for new homes because they had been chased so much.

The ten remaining squirrels could share the food store comfortably and Sciurus came to know them all well. They rarely chased one another because now they were few enough to have plenty of food and nest-holes, and each squirrel knew his position in relation to the other members of the group. In the event of a dispute the two squirrels would merely indicate their intentions and the weaker one withdrew before it got to the stage of chasing. Normally the sight of a stronger animal approaching was enough, but sometimes a squirrel was tempted to stay longer. The stronger animal would then signal its intentions by fluffing out its tail, narrowing its eyes, moving its ears forward

and chattering its teeth. The weaker would respond by relaxing its tail hairs, opening its eyes wide, laying its ears back and emitting a squealing growl.

If the strange male, now a member of the group, merely looked at Sciurus, he usually just got out of his way, but once Sciurus tried to hold his ground, because he had found a big acorn. The new squirrel narrowed his eyes into slits and pricked his ears forward so that puffs of white hair showed on them. Sciurus growled and scratched at him as he approached, hoping to keep the acorn, but it was no use, he had to drop the acorn and run. The new squirrel didn't always have it his own way, because one of the other males was stronger and could take things from any of the nine other squirrels in the group whenever he wanted.

As the weather got colder in November, the drey became damp and the wind blew through it. Sciurus and his brother went to join their mother in the hole in the leaning beech.

They found that it was comfortable and warm, and they were not alone; two other females were also living there with two more young squirrels. The two adult males and the new squirrel usually lived together in a neighbouring beech. A large branch had fallen off a long time ago and where it had been attached a hollow had rotted in the trunk. The males had built themselves a drey in this sheltered spot. These ten squirrels, of whom Sciurus was one, rarely ventured far from the circle of beech trees fringed with oaks which made up their home area.

Their patch of woodland of about one hectare was bordered by the marsh and grassland, and there were broad avenues of trees extending to the north, south and east. Sciurus soon learned why the squirrels didn't go outside the area. One day he wanted to go south, back to the wood with the chestnut trees. He had been foraging in the leaf litter near some birch trees, not really paying attention to where he was heading, when he noticed that he was at the base of the hollow oak. This reminded him that there had been some large nuts beyond this tree, but he was fearful of going there again. He climbed a little way up the tree and found a patch on the trunk below the first branch which was heavily gnawed by squirrels and had a strong smell. He chipped a little bit out of the trunk with his teeth and then looked towards the beech with branches that bent down to the ground. This tree was on the way to the chestnut wood. Warily he came down the oak and hesitatingly went over to the beech. He cut a small chip from one of the branches lying on the ground, and left a little pool of urine. Nothing had happened thus far, so he

went along the ground following a well-used squirrel track through some ivy growing below a sycamore tree. The track went under some small holly bushes, where it was very dark. On the other side he came to some chestnut husks. He sniffed around amongst the leaf litter until he found what he was looking for: the beautiful sweet scent of a chestnut. When he dug it up he noticed that the top end had been chewed out, so he knew that another squirrel had buried it. He was just about to peel it when a squirrel appeared, coming straight for him down the trunk of the chestnut tree.

Sciurus could see from its narrowed eyes, exposed white ear puffs and deliberate manner that he was going to be chased just as he had been before, so he didn't wait for it to get any nearer, but stuffed the chestnut into his mouth and raced back along the squirrel track until he got past the hollow oak. Once there he sat on a log and ate his prize.

From this experience Sciurus learned not to go beyond the trees with gnawed patches which smelled strongly of urine because they marked the edge of the home area which belonged to his group of squirrels. The neighbouring squirrels were always very unfriendly and usually chased him, so he risked going past the marking points only when he had some special reason, such as going to get a chestnut, and when he thought he could get away with it.

While eating the chestnut, he bit on something very hard, but swallowed it before he knew what it was. His jaw felt a bit sore on one side as he chewed more of the chestnut pulp. He had lost one of his milk teeth. At the age of four months squirrels lose their four milk teeth. All Sciurus's other teeth would be permanent, including his big front incisors. These had to grow all the time, because opening nuts and acorns made them wear down very quickly.

It was nearly eleven o'clock the next day when the squirrels first started coming out. There had been a hard frost during the night, and the weak December sun melted only the ice crystals on the sunny side of the grass tussocks. Having been cramped in the hole all night, the squirrels underneath the heap of bodies complained and pushed their way through the others, squeaking and growling. The seven occupants came out of the hole, one after the other, and sat in the sun on branches near the hole. Sciurus preened his brother, gently scraping the surface of the skin on the back of his head with his sharp front teeth, pulling off loose bits and combing out fleas. They had both moulted their baby fur

and now had warm, silvery-grey winter coats. Sciurus preened his own coat, spending nearly half an hour licking, scratching and combing it. It was important for him to look after his coat so that it kept him dry and did not become too infested with fleas and lice. Then he caught hold of his tail in his forepaws and preened it all the way up. It also had to be kept in good condition so that he could use it for balancing while running through the trees, and for signalling to other squirrels.

When he had finished, Sciurus wiped his mouth on the branches and ran down the tree to a place where he knew some acorns were buried. He found one almost immediately, dug it up and took it to a nearby stump, where he peeled and ate it. He was just about to get another one, when he saw a squirrel run along a branch in one of the beech trees and disappear behind the trunk. Sciurus saw the squirrel very clearly because there were no leaves on the trees now, and the squirrel flagged its bushy tail over its back as it dashed along the branches.

Sciurus knew instantly that this meant danger, so he bounded to the nearest tree, which was a birch, and clung on to the trunk. He could hear the danger approaching, but he could not move to a safer place in the tall trees for fear of being seen. It was a man with a gun. Sciurus kept himself hidden behind the trunk, and quietly scrambled round as the man walked past, only about a metre away. Sciurus didn't know when it was safe to move again, because he was still hiding behind the trunk. He had to wait until he saw another squirrel in the trees move before he knew the danger had passed.

In general, life was very casy for Sciurus. Most of the time he slept in the nest, often not coming out at all on cold windy days. He liked warm, damp, windless days best of all, for then it was easy to find things by scent. There were all sorts of interesting smells on branches, where birds had settled and where squirrels had run, or wiped their mouths. It was also easy to find acorns and beechnuts buried in the leaf litter. It took him only a few minutes to eat enough to satisfy him each day.

He had few worries until one day early in January. Many squirrels were out that day, even though a cold east wind was blowing. Sciurus came out to discover what was going on. He found that there were a lot of squirrels running through the trees making an unusual noise: "chuff . . . chuff . . . chuff . . .". He could tell from the scent left in their footsteps that some were strangers, and that they were adult males. A flurry of snow crystals stung his nose and ears, so Sciurus returned to the warmth and safety of the hole in the leaning beech. All the other squirrels were still in the hole, except his mother. She was out in the trees at the centre of the activity, because she was preparing for another family.

5

Out in the Cold

During the next two weeks, Sciurus had to keep out of the way of more large adult males which came into the home area. He didn't understand what was going on, but, like his mother, the other females also mated and were to have families later in the year. After the two weeks had passed, the same lazy life returned, although it became less easy to find acorns. The store was being used up and Sciurus had to spend more time finding enough to eat. One day he was awakened by an unusual light coming into the tree-hole. When he put his head out he was greeted by a dazzling picture of sun shining on snow. He climbed out on to the branch, slipping on its icy surface and knocking off a lump of snow in the process, which fell and

made a little hole in the featureless carpet below. He climbed down the tree and carefully walked out into the snow, his feet sinking through its crust.

He hopped across to a log, jumped on to it and sat there looking at the scene around him. He walked along the top, pushing snow off with his nose, jumped down and began to look for something to eat. He dug a hole in the snow and pulled out some beech leaves. He enlarged the hole and foraged around in the beech leaves until he found a beechnut and ate it. He walked off a little way to a place where there were usually some acorns, and sniffed around over the snow until he smelled something familiar.

He dug straight down to a large acorn, and sat beside the hole to eat it. He left the shell lying on the snow before hopping towards a tree stump.

Something scared him before he got there. Lying in the snow was a dead robin. He stretched forward to look, pushing the end of his tail over his right ear, just in case there was danger present. There were squirrel tracks near the robin, and leaves which the robin had pulled out from under the stump while searching for food. The bird must have been caught by a squirrel which had cracked the robin's head open and eaten the contents. Sciurus sniffed the dead bird, climbed on to the stump to make sure that there were no predators around, and then foraged for some more beechnuts.

In the afternoon, as the sun went low in the sky, it became very cold in the blue shadows of the trees. Sciurus had eaten enough and was looking forward to the warmth of the nest-hole. His mother was waiting for him on the branch below the hole but, instead of a greeting, she chattered her teeth and chased him down the tree. He waited there for a while and then went back. His mother growled loudly and chattered her teeth from within the hole. He could not sleep there that night. During the previous few days the other females had moved out, and now it was Sciurus's turn. His mother was about to have another family, and no squirrels were to be allowed in the nest until these young had grown big.

What was Sciurus to do? There was snow on the ground, night was approaching, and it was beginning to freeze hard. He was too frightened to go to the males' drey, so he went to an old woodpecker hole in a neighbouring beech. As he looked in the hole, a female inside growled and scratched at his face. He climbed up and crossed to another beech on the edge of the circle. A long time ago he had been in a drey there, sitting in a fork at the top of the trunk. As he approached, his claws made scratching sounds on the trunk and the occupant of the drey growled loudly at him. He knew he couldn't stay there either. He came down the tree and was sitting on a log, unsure what to do, when suddenly he had to duck and run away, because a mistlethrush swooped at him. She had a nest in the tree nearby and rightly regarded him as a potential egg-stealer.

The experience of being swooped on by a bird may have reminded him of the old drey in the oak where he had been struck by the sparrowhawk. He headed for the oak, climbed up and cautiously approached the drey. It was dark and it smelled, but no squirrels growled

at him. He pushed his way through the collapsed entrance and found it damp, cold and musty inside. A woodmouse had left some nutshells on the floor. He turned round inside several times, making the cavity fit his rounded body, and pushed leaves into holes in the walls with his nose and paws. He settled down to rest but could feel the cold penetrating to his bones. After a while he heard scratching noises outside and he quickly poked his head out to see what it was. It was his brother and one of the other juveniles coming to join him. They had been thrown out by his mother as well. They came in and preened one another. The three bodies together would be enough to keep out the cold that night.

Sciurus didn't sleep well. He kept hearing noises and felt uncomfortable. All three squirrels fidgeted through the night, pushing under each other to try and keep warm. In the morning there was a crisp frost on top of the snow and they came out as soon as the sun shone on the drey. They sat together on a branch outside, preening themselves, and soon found why their night had been so disturbed. Their fur was full of fleas. The fleas had been waiting in the drey for the warmth of squirrel bodies, and had crept out of debris at the bottom of the nest feeling very hungry.

The squirrels spent a long time putting their fur in order, catching and eating as many fleas as they could. Sciurus was preened by the other two, then he preened his brother's head and back, catching a lot of fleas. When he got tired of this job he pulled his body over the top of his brother, lying there in the sun. His brother peeped out from under his flank. For a while they romped in the branches as they had done when they were small, but eventually stopped as there was work to be done.

Sciurus could see that there were a few leaves

hanging on to twigs which had been left after the autumn gales. These leaves were crisp and dry in the cold sunny air. He climbed out on to the fine branches, clinging on tightly in case they broke, and stretched forward to pluck some leaves with his teeth. He bundled these into a parcel by stroking them with his fore-paws as he held them in his mouth. Then he ran to the drey and pushed them into a hole in the side. He turned round a couple of times before coming out to collect some more. This time he came down the tree and found some dry leaves which had blown into a cleft between two roots at the base of the tree where the snow had not covered them. He bundled these up in the same way and took them into the drey. With the help of the other two squirrels it was soon repaired and made dry and warm inside.

Later, while the squirrels were out finding acorns, a west wind began to blow and clouds covered the sun. The wood became full of dripping sounds as the snow thawed. The squirrels went back to the drey to sleep.

The next morning Sciurus found enough acorns very quickly because most of the snow had melted and it was a warm damp day. His brother had been slow getting up that morning and as the days passed he became weaker because he had become infected with a disease.

One warm day late in February they both sat outside the drey. Sciurus preened his brother for a while before coming down the tree. He stretched and yawned, before heading for a tree across the stream where he had seen some squirrels the day before.

Sciurus had wondered what they had been doing there. He went past the base of the leaning beech, in which his mother was tending her new family, to a large oak by the swamp. He waited for a while, surveying the open space he had to cross, then ran towards an old timber bridge spanning the marsh. But he became scared halfway there and dashed back to the oak. Once near the oak he regained his nerve and turned to run to the marsh and across the bridge to the safety of a sycamore tree on the other side. He went on through the trees to the elm where he had seen the squirrels. Here, high up in the branches, he found bundles of flowers which were good to eat. But he wasn't able to stay there long because one of the young males that lived in this area came and chased him. Later in the day, when he returned to the drey, his brother was not there. Sciurus did not see him again.

6

Some Flowers are Good to Eat

It was April, now and it was getting warmer. Birds sang and buds showed green in the trees. Yellow kingcups flowered in the marsh. During the past few weeks, Sciurus had increasingly been supplementing his acorn diet with more buds. Flower buds on the rowan trees had been the first and squirrels had eaten most of these. After that they began to eat buds on the young sycamores.

Sciurus had been up early in the morning, eating acorns and examining new smells on the branches and stumps on the ground. He bundled up some dry leaves, intending to put a new lining on the drey, but feeling exhilarated by the spring air he was easily distracted. He hopped playfully around with his load and

blundered into a fallen branch. He leaped into the air, scattering the bundle in all directions. Then, after a noisy landing on dry leaves, he flicked his tail and rushed around in a circle.

He saw a smooth hollow beside the branch and went into it for a dust bath, turning on his side and scuffing dust over himself. He may have been trying to remove an itchy feeling on his skin. He rolled and tumbled inside the hollow and then pulled himself out and rolled over and over down the hill amongst the dead leaves. He got up and did two little jumps in the air, then tore round in a circle again, flapping his tail. A rabbit came over to see what all the commotion was about, but Sciurus ignored it and ran past up a small birch tree, where he found some strange smells on the trunk near the top. A squirrel he did not recognize had been there. The trunk had many bite marks in the bark from which sap was pouring and splashing on the branches below.

Sciurus came down the birch and climbed the big oak by the marsh. Its fat buds looked like small fruit from below. He went up to the buds at the very top of the tree and broke off a twig which had five buds on it. He carried this to a place where he could sit properly and turned the twig round in his hands. Yellowish-green catkins were poking out from between the bud scales. He bit these off with his teeth and ate them. When he had finished the five buds he went to collect another twig. Soon the ground below was littered with discarded twigs.

The oaks provided the most reliable year-round food source for Sciurus. There was nearly always something to eat either on the trees or under them. But one day in early May an event occurred which moulded his whole future. He was now fully grown and had put on a lot of weight since the end of March. He was beginning to act in a superior manner, because there were a lot of baby squirrels around, and he found he could always get what he wanted by chasing them away. If one found an acorn, or a tasty fungus, all Sciurus needed to do was run at the young squirrel, and the prize was his.

On a morning in early May he woke as he usually did about half past five and found it was very cold outside. When he climbed up to the top of the oak he saw that the oak leaves, which had previously been shining pale green miniatures of the grown leaf, were now limp and dull. As the day wore on the green stems drooped and the leaves turned black. There had been a late frost. It had killed all the leaves near the tops of the trees and had killed the female flowers as well. Very few acorns would grow that year. Sciurus would have to leave the wood and seek a new home before winter.

He came down the tree looking for other shoots to eat. He went on an excursion into the chestnut wood and found another tree new to him. It had a craggy bark which flaked off as he climbed up and there were tender shoots growing out of large sticky buds. It was a horse chestnut tree. Some of the shoots had flower buds growing and Sciurus broke these off and ate them. He also ate the tender leaf stems. Not many buds were left since the squirrels living in the area had also been eating them. Few flowers meant there would be hardly any horse chestnuts that year either.

Sciurus left when he saw one of the squirrels approaching, and slowly made his way back to his own part of the wood. On the way he found some bluebells growing out of the woodland floor. He bit one off, but it was sticky and he dropped it, and wiped his mouth on a fallen branch. Squirrels do not like bluebells, or their bulbs, perhaps because they contain a poison.

A few days later Sciurus went to a small oak tree on the edge of the wood. The sun was shining brightly and pale green leaves had unfolded from branches low down on the trunk. These had been sheltered from the frost. Many of the leaves had holes eaten in them and Sciurus sniffed around amongst them. He picked off some caterpillars which looked just like sticks. They could fool birds, but squirrels hunting with their noses could easily find them.

At the end of a branch a beautiful oak apple had grown. Sciurus plucked this prize gall and took it back to the trunk. He split it open and ate the grubs inside, dropping the pieces on to the delicate bracken fronds below which had also escaped the frost. He went out again to look for more galls and found some juicy currant galls growing on old male catkins. He opened these while some iridescent moths with long antennae danced like mayflies over the leaf tips and cast shadows on his body.

Near the trunk, higher up, he found something quite new. It was a wood pigeon's nest with two white eggs resting in it. He quickly picked one up in his mouth, but as he did so, he tipped the flimsy nest so the other egg fell and smashed on the ground. He went to a vantage point, egg in mouth, where he sat holding it in his forepaws. He cracked it open making smacking noises as he ate the slimy contents. Bits of yolk stuck to his chin and sides of his mouth, and when he had finished he wiped his mouth all along the branch.

It was a long time before the leaves in the tops of the oaks began to grow properly, because there were many caterpillars in the trees, which ate the leaves as they grew. On very still days

Sciurus could hear the gentle hissing sound of their droppings falling on to the dry leaf litter below. When the caterpillars were ready to turn into crysalids they dropped from the treetops on long silk threads. One day in mid-May there was a strong wind and many caterpillars were falling or being blown out of the trees. All the birds and squirrels congregated below the trees, waiting expectantly for the best caterpillars. There was a rush and much quarrelling when large caterpillars fell. As the wind died down Sciurus walked slowly over the wood floor amongst some grass tussocks. He put his nose to the ground and found many more caterpillars. It was on this rich diet that he quickly became a healthy adult.

7

Hunting for a Mate

Later in May, Sciurus had a strange, uneasy feeling when he came out of the drey in the morning. Another strong wind was blowing dead leaves over the woodland floor and thrushes were searching for falling caterpillars. Sciurus went down to join them. He felt uneasy because he could not be sure that he was safe from predators. The wind roaring through the trees and blowing everything about made it difficult to hear or see their furtive movements. But this did not fully account for his uneasy feeling. He stood up on his hind legs to look around him. He revealed his white belly which could easily be seen across the wood, while his bushy tail blew around in the wind. He could see some of the other squirrels he knew.

When a flurry of leaves blew up in a gust of wind he saw, at the edge of the circle of beeches near the hollow oak, the white shaft of another squirrel's belly as it was standing up to look around. It was a large squirrel and Sciurus could see it was a male by the way it carried its tail. The end was held out straight, unlike a female who usually lets the end flop over. The male ran into the area with a lolloping gait and then two more appeared behind him. They seemed to be following the first, but also played and chased one another. They worked their way through the home area, visiting the marking points and went up to all the resident squirrels they saw. The big male came straight over near to where Sciurus was standing. He stopped

by a fallen branch and sat displaying aggressive signals by paddling his hind feet on the ground and making loud rasping noises as he gnawed large chunks out of the branch.

Sciurus knew he was going to be chased, so was ready to run when the stranger sprang towards him. After gnawing a chunk out of the stump Sciurus had been sitting on, the squirrel went off to one of the females. Instead of running away, she went on catching caterpillars, apparently ignoring him. He followed her as she foraged in the litter and then went off to a marking point.

The wood seemed to be full of squirrels, running this way and that, some coming to look at the newcomers, and running away in fear. The newcomers chased all the young males they saw. Then, all of a sudden, the wood became quiet again. The three squirrels had gone north out of the other side of the home area and all the residents were sitting quietly in the trees. Only a thrush and wind-blown leaves were active on the forest floor.

Sciurus went to visit one of the marking posts, and found some large chunks had been gnawed out and that the patch smelled strongly of urine. He followed the route taken by the visiting males. They had left patches of scent on branches as they went. He went into some birch trees on the border of the area occupied by an adjoining group of squirrels, but was afraid to go much farther. He ran up and down the trunk flapping his tail, jumped into an oak, came down and ran back home along a squirrel path on the ground. He was starting to violate group boundaries himself.

During the next few weeks more males came through the home area and Sciurus slowly extended his movements, leaving scent on new marking points he encountered. He learned which were the best routes to follow through the trees and along the ground, so that he always knew where to run if chased by a predator, or by a resident squirrel. He was grown up and was looking for females who were ready to mate. He discovered which females were going to breed that year by their scent when he followed them. He also learned which males would chase him and which ones he could chase, by approaching them and seeing how they reacted to mild threats. All the squirrels chased the many new juveniles.

Three weeks after the first males had come through the wood Sciurus went on a long excursion. He had now moulted his grey winter fur and had a greeny-brown coat, which matched the colour of tree trunks. On his feet and flanks he had flashes of orangey-brown fur which blended with the leaf litter on the ground. He even had a dark streak down the middle of his white belly which was unusual. These colours made him very difficult to see when he went through the deep shadows of the wood. He went south through the wood with the chestnut trees and into some hollies. From there he went to a sycamore and crossed to a birch on the other side of the stream. He kept sniffing the branches as he went, and when he came to an ash tree he smelled something which excited him. The female in the area was ready to be mated.

He ran through the trees when he heard her calling, but found that he was not alone. Many other males responded by running towards the calls, all making the strange "chuff . . . chuff . . . chuff . . ." noise that he had heard during the winter when his mother was mated. When he got there he found that the female was sitting at the end of a dead branch. The big male which he had seen earlier was busy chasing away all the other males as they approached. Sciurus couldn't even get near because other males, older than himself, chased him. He resorted to chasing away the smallest males he could find. After a while the female ran past the male and rapidly went through the trees followed by all her suitors. Sciurus got

closer to the female this time, but was quickly chased away by the old males when they caught up.

Sciurus then chased a youngster and chewed a long strip of bark off a branch in frustration. Underneath the bark he found the wood was wet and tasted sweet, so he ate some of the growing layers under the bark. As he was doing this an older squirrel rushed at him. Sciurus was not ready for this and lost his footing. He clutched desperately at the leaves, but they just tore, so he spread his four legs and tail out and sailed down to the ground, nine metres below. When he landed there was a loud 'plop' noise, as the air trapped under him escaped; it had formed a cushion which saved him from getting hurt. He returned home disappointed.

More weeks had passed and it was now early July. Sciurus was tired, hungry and frustrated. He had been making long journeys each day looking for a mate, but each time he found a female, there were larger males already there who chased him away. He hadn't had time to eat properly, so he had lost a lot of weight. Today there was a hazy sun; the air was close and smelled of honeysuckle and stinkhorn fungus. There was no wind and he could hear the hum of flies hovering in the clearings. This time his quest took him north along a track through some tall bracken, and wound past a small pine plantation and amongst white silver birch stems, to an isolated chestnut. As he went on, through a young beech plantation and birch grove, he heard a female calling. He ran over some open grassy patches to get to the tall beech where her call came from. He found a patch of her scent on a branch and this told him that she was ready to be mated.

This time he was the first male to find her, but she was most unfriendly, because she was afraid of Sciurus, and scratched and growled at him as he approached. She was a young squirrel like himself and was breeding later than the others. Two more young males came up the tree, but Sciurus was determined to keep his place. He turned and chattered his teeth at the nearest. This one didn't run away, so Sciurus chased him. While he was doing this, the female ran past him, went up the tree and into a hole. Sciurus rushed after her but she growled and scratched at him when he tried to follow. He stayed outside on the trunk chasing the other males off, but eventually could restrain himself no longer and made an excited "shuck.. shuck..shuck.." noise to let her know he was about to enter the hole, then he rushed through the entrance. There she allowed him to mate her, having lost some of her fear.

Sciurus came out of the nest and preened himself while the female called within "chuck-pooeee . . . chuck-pooeee . . .". He stayed there for a while, chasing the other males when they came too close. Then he set off for home.

8
Exhaustion

As Sciurus left the female the midday sun went behind some dark clouds. The air was heavy and still. He climbed down the beech and began to feel hungry and tired as he crossed the open grassy clearing. The air was rank with stinkhorn fungus. He followed the scent and on the edge of the clearing, he found an egg-like immature stinkhorn fungus poking through the wood-grass nearby. He bit through the jelly coat and ate some of the compressed fungus within. After walking a bit farther he came to a stump and found the remains of an old horse chestnut. It had been buried last year and a hungry squirrel had recently discarded it, after rasping some of the hard flesh. As Sciurus was eating it there was a roll of thunder and he ran up the nearby birch. He was exhausted from the morning exertions and from weeks of long journeys seeking a mate.

The birch grove took a further toll of his flagging energies because it was hard work crossing from tree to tree using the slender branches which sagged under his weight. He

was afraid of travelling on the ground because the thunder had scared him. He stopped after a while to eat some of the birch catkins which were hanging in the tops of the trees, when his attention was drawn to a curious rending sound. It was a squirrel tearing bark off a young beech in the plantation, dropping the bits on the ground and eating the white flesh revealed below. Sciurus was angered by its presence and chased the squirrel, which ran a little way off, where it continued stripping bark. He heard more chasing nearby and saw two more squirrels, both furiously stripping bark. One was a young female, born that spring, which used to live in his part of the wood.

All the young squirrels in Sciurus's home area had been chased by the adults, because it was overcrowded with youngsters. Even the stronger young had chased the weaker ones. Some had died. Others, like this female, had gone looking for a new home. She had been chased wherever she went until she came to the beech plantation. Soon after arriving she had tried to settle by building a summer drey, which merely consisted of a flimsy platform of leafy twigs.

There were no squirrels to chase her because the plantation had not provided enough food or nest sites during the winter. For the same reason, she could not stay long, so had little chance of survival. Shortly after coming there, her situation became hopeless, as six other young squirrels, also chased out of their home areas, had entered the plantation. Each of them wanted to live in the area on his own. They tried to drive the others out, using all the aggressive signals they knew, especially tearing bark with their teeth, and chasing. Made hungry by their exertions and frustrated by their hopeless situation, they soon began to eat the sweet growing layers of bark revealed after they had torn off the surface. They were filling their stomachs at the same time as they were aggressively breaking the bark. This is the only time of year when living bark is easy to remove and squirrels can eat it. By eating the bark they were destroying what homes they might have had because they were killing the trees.

As Sciurus watched, one of these squirrels was chased down a tree into some bracken and he heard a crashing sound, which made the other squirrels call. Then he saw what had happened. A black cat came out carrying the limp body of the squirrel. The others would soon die, killed by the cat, a fox, or by sickness made worse by their bark diet. In America, where grey squirrels first came from, social outcasts such as these are killed by their natural

predators or disease long before they get to the stage of destroying their own environment by eating bark.

There was a loud clap of thunder and it poured with rain. Sciurus left the beech plantation, but still had a long way to go home. He kept himself fairly dry by shaking the raindrops off as they stuck to his fur. He soon came to an iron fence beside a man-made path. This went in the right direction, so he walked along the top for some distance. Eventually he came to the small pine plantation, by which time the storm had passed.

The sun came out and the air was fresh again. Water sparkled on the tips of the pine needles.

These fell off in heavy showers as he climbed high up in the branches. Some green pine cones grew here, and he worked hard to twist a cone off its stalk. He chewed through the bases of the scales and ate the white seeds developing inside. After a while his jaw ached from gnawing cones, but the rain had cleared the air and he felt refreshed. He tried to wipe the sticky resin off his face and then came down the tree to re-join the squirrel track. He was now on familiar ground and lolloped his way home through the bracken, getting very wet as he pushed through some grass which had been laid flat by the rain.

When he got back to his home area, he found it looked very different. Light was pouring into the woodland floor where it had always been in shadow. The leaning beech had broken in two. The trunk that had been damaged by lightning a long time ago had finally been destroyed by a thunderstorm. It had split just where the squirrel's nest was. Sciurus went to his drey and curled up for a long sleep.

9

Looking for a New Home

During the next few weeks Sciurus rested. Very little seemed to be happening to the squirrel population. He fed mainly in the tops of beech trees where female flowers were beginning to develop into nuts. He ate the soft growing layers inside. Sometimes, when he had finished eating, he came down the tree and found a sunny spot on the ground where he flopped down to warm himself. In August the nutshells became hard and no longer had any edible layers inside. Very few had fertile nuts in them this year. Instead of putting on fat for the coming winter, he continued to lose weight. His mother caught a virus disease and became paralysed in her hindquarters, so that she could hardly climb a tree. She died soon after.

After her death, Sciurus tried to join the males living in the neighbouring beech, but they chased him whenever he came near the trunk. He went over to the fringe of oak trees on the edge of the home area. The acorns were nearly fully grown and were becoming edible. He chose one tree which had the sweetest tasting acorns, but had to search several branches for each acorn he found. Because of the spring frost only a few acorns had grown. He went out into a grassy area and found a little oak tree about fifteen centimetres tall. It had been stored as an acorn last year, but had not been prevented from germinating when the squirrel had bitten out the growing point. Sciurus found the old acorn attached to the stem and ate it, leaving the little oak tree to grow and extend the woodland for later generations of squirrels.

At the end of August Sciurus found he was spending too much time looking for food. He was restless, and one day he set off to look for somewhere else to live. He set off south past the hollow oak, perhaps because he still hankered after the chestnut wood. He lolloped to the beech and along the squirrel track through the ivy and hollies to the first chestnut. He climbed round the trunk and found the marking point. It was well marked so he knew squirrels still

Some of the things Sciurus Eats

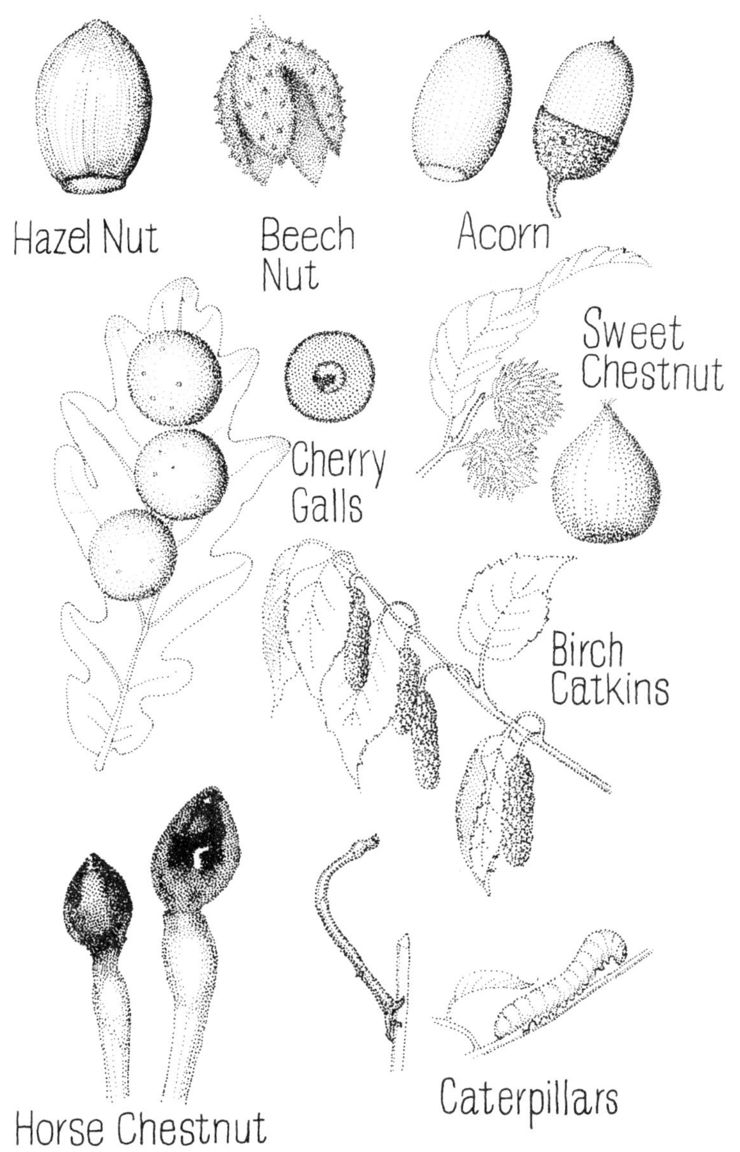

lived there. He left his own marks by chipping some more bark off and then went on along the path in the middle of the avenue of trees. Two large males chased him on the way, but he avoided them and kept going. He climbed the hollies at the end of the wood and crossed the stream. He made slow progress through the scrubby birches and sycamores until he came to a big lime tree. This was as far as he had been before and there were no more trees for some distance, so now he had to go on the ground.

He ran down the lime and soon found a rabbit track continuing in a southerly direction. It took him along a winding course through elder bushes and stinging nettles. The path ended when he came to some rabbit holes so he climbed up a small elm to look around. He felt very vulnerable because it was difficult to tell which branch led on to the next tree. The first one he tried had such a big gap that it was too far to jump. He tried one higher up and leaped across, but he lost his balance in flight because he had moulted most of his tail hairs and the new ones hadn't grown yet. He crashed into the next tree making a loud noise – if there were any predators around, they would surely be searching for him now.

But, instead of meeting any predators, he

came to an open gap in the trees where he saw things roaring past at tremendous speed, making a terrible noise. He could see some larger trees on the other side, and decided to cross the gap. The surface was very hard and smelled strange. He looked across to the other side, but had to run back as another thing dashed past. He sat on a post for a while, not knowing what to do. He couldn't turn back, and he couldn't live in the small elms. He looked across the road for some time and got ready to make a dash for it. It was all quiet, nothing seemed to be coming, so down the post he went. As he got on to the road, a car suddenly appeared over the brow of the hill. It was too late now, so he continued to run until the car came very close, towering over him. Then his nerve faltered and he started to run back, but then he seemed to be running into the path of the car, so he quickly turned again. It all went dark in the shadow of the car and he felt a stinging pain. Then the car was gone and Sciurus made a blind dash to the trees on the other side. He sat on the first branch and, when he preened his tail, soon found what had happened. He had lost the tip.

He crossed into the next tree where he found an old stockdove's nest in a hollow branch, and he went inside to rest. Early the next day he got up and sat in the sun preening for a long time, trying to catch some of the fleas and mites that had crawled on to him during the night. He went down the tree and foraged around for some food on the ground. There he found some earwigs to eat under a piece of elder bark. As he was hunting for more in some ivy, a bumblebee buzzed at him from under the leaves. He jumped with fright, shook his tail, purred, stamped his feet, ran up a tree and called.

He heard other squirrels calling a long way off in reply. After a while he set off in their direction along a belt of larch trees. As he got closer he saw there were many big trees, and it looked a good place to live. He found the squirrels in a large oak tree on a hill surrounded by other large trees of various kinds. There were a lot of acorns. The spring frost had hit only the valleys where cold air had poured in from the surrounding open pastures. He visited a marking point on the trunk and found that it hadn't been used much recently. He left his mark there and then climbed up the tree. The other squirrels came to look at him and a young male chased after him. But Sciurus went up into the branches and collected an acorn. He took it down and buried it carefully in the ground.

After storing acorns for a while with the other squirrels, they took less notice of him, although he had to avoid the young male each time he passed him on the trunk. He heard other squirrels calling in a tree about a hundred metres away and replied. That night he slept in a drey on his own. He found it in a holly tree and made it soft inside by lining it with bark from a nearby redwood tree.

There was no large male in this group of squirrels. He had died during the summer, and the young male didn't chase Sciurus enough to make him want to move any farther. During the next few weeks he was very active, eating some acorns and storing others. Eventually he was accepted into this new group of squirrels, and together they chased away other migrating squirrels as they came in along the band of larch trees. Sciurus put on weight and grew a beautiful new plume to his tail, much thicker than before. He could always be recognized by the funny tassel of hair at the tip of his tail where the car had broken it.

10

Sciurus the Leader

Many things are likely to happen to Sciurus before he dies. Having survived for more than a year, he is probably sufficiently experienced to avoid predators, and has become immune to the diseases which sometimes kill young squirrels. If we returned to the wood in three years' time it is quite likely we would see Sciurus. He would then be a large male, perhaps the leading male of the group, and able to choose the best nests to live in and chase whom he pleased in the home area. He would have a line of pale fur on his eyelids which would make him look very mean when he narrowed his eyes, before chasing another squirrel. His ears would be more ragged from fights and he would have a thick grey bushy tail (still with a tassel on the end), no longer the thin, brown-streaked tail of a young squirrel.

During the breeding seasons in January and June he would perhaps return to the wood where he was born, looking for females ready to mate. He would find that the beech, where the males had had their nest, had broken off like the leaning beech, and the wood floor grown into a tangle of bracken, brambles and birch trees where the dead beeches had let the light come in. He would find the elm over the marsh dead from the ravages of Dutch elm disease, and young beeches planted to replace the dead trees (with protective plastic sleeves put around the trunks by men to prevent young squirrels from damaging the bark). He would see a strong growth of oak trees flourishing in the grassland around the edge of the wood. He may have planted some of these when he helped to build his first winter food store.

If Sciurus is lucky, or very wary of the black cat and of men with guns, he may live until he is five, or even seven years old. Eventually he will die – maybe after becoming sick at a time of food shortage or by being taken by a predator, when engrossed once too often in retrieving a large chestnut or chasing another squirrel. We should not be sorry when he dies, because his death will mean that another squirrel can live in the wood where he now lives, and his body will be used gladly by other animals, whether crow, stoat, fox, cat, beetle or fly. An oak may even grow stronger when his remains decay into the soil.

Reading List

THE GREY SQUIRREL A. D. Middleton, Sidgwick and Jackson, London, 1931.

GREY SQUIRRELS M. Shorten, Animals of Britain No.5, Sunday Times Book Publications, London, 1962.

RED SQUIRRELS M. Shorten, Animals of Britain No.6, Sunday Times Book Publications, London, 1962.

SQUIRRELS M. Shorten, Collins, London, 1954.

THE HANDBOOK OF BRITISH MAMMALS G. B. Corbet and H. N. Southern, Blackwell, Oxford, 1977.

THE WORLD OF THE GREY SQUIRREL F. S. Barkalow and M. Shorten, Lippincott, New York, 1973.